Rudolf Steiner

Anthroposophy: An Introduction

Supplementary Materials

Edited by Frederick Amrine

Work in Light of the Christmas Conference 10

CONTENTS

General Introduction:

The Christmas Conference

"At the end of 1923 the Christmas Conference took place in the *Schreinerei*, the carpentry workshop near the site of the Goetheanum which had been burnt down one year earlier. … First of all it was Rudolf Steiner's attempts to bring together all the national societies and groups, founded during the course of 1923, in the General Anthroposophical Society. This was at the same time to be the bearer of all work in the sciences, arts and practical activities. The School of Spiritual Science became the center of the Society and all anthroposophical work. Rudolf Steiner had taken the self-sacrificing decision to assume the direction of the Society and School himself, so that the unity for which he had striven could really arise. Through this decision the whole spiritual impulse which he represented became karmically linked to the renewed Society: Anthroposophical Movement and Anthroposophical Society were to be, he said, from now on forever one. Rudolf Steiner wanted to erect, together with all his pupils and co-workers, a living social foundation which in the future would be capable of letting the stream of spiritual life, that had worked in him so far, flow into civilization." (p. 120)

"The Christmas Conference of 1923 was an attempt to bring about, as it were, the incarnation of Anthroposophy in a manner befitting the Spirit of the Age. The vessel for this incarnation was to be the newly founded Anthroposophical Society. From this, as center, Anthroposophy was to become manifest in new creative activities in cultural life. The Society received a task as noble as it was difficult. While being completely open to the world, it must also work from an esoteric basis and this meant that as a community it had to tread the path of inner development. All true inner development leads through trials: that is, through intensive confrontation with one's own destiny. Herewith we touch on what was to be the fundamental theme, not only of the year 1924, but for the whole seven-year period from 1924 to 1930: *Knowledge of the collective karma of anthroposophists.*" (p. 2)

"The Christmas Conference was in more than one sense a karmic event. But the word *karmic* received its greatest importance from the future. For through this event Rudolf Steiner, in sublime freedom, built *new* karma. In another way, too, this Christmas week was filled with destiny for, as Rudolf Steiner continually emphasized, it demanded to be carried further in new deeds." (p. 3)

"… one can describe the Christmas Conference as Rudolf Steiner's attempt to accomplish the new beginnings of the Mysteries. The Mystery Deed in the narrow sense was the laying of the spiritual Foundation Stone on Christmas morning. In the form of his all-embracing, highly concentrated meditative words, Rudolf Steiner laid the kernel of Anthroposophy in the hearts of those present." (p. 121)

From Hans Peter van Manen, *Twin Roads to the New Millennium: the Christmas Conference and the Karma of the Anthroposophical Society* (Forest Row: Rudolf Steiner Press, 2014)

GA 260; *The Christmas Conference for the Foundation of the General Anthroposophical Society 1923/1924: The Laying of the Foundation Stone: Lectures and Addresses: Discussion of the Statutes: Dornach, 24 December 1923 to 1 January 1924* (Hudson, NY: Anthroposophic Press, 1990).

GA 233; *World History and the Mysteries in the Light of Anthroposophy*. Trans. George Adams and Dorothy Osmond. London: Rudolf Steiner Press, 1997. [December 26-29, 1923] [1]

Frederick Amrine, ed. GA 233; *World History and the Mysteries in the Light of Anthroposophy. Vol. 2: Supplemental Materials*. ([Amazon:]) Keryx, 2020.

Frederick Amrine. GA 233; *World History and the Mysteries in the Light of Anthroposophy. Vol. 3: Commentary*. ([Amazon:]) Keryx, 2020.

GA 291 [excerpt]; "The Hierarchies and the Essence of the Rainbow." Ed. and trans. Frederick Amrine. ([Amazon:]) Keryx, 2020. [January 4, 1924]

GA 260 and GA 260a [excerpts]; *The Foundation Stone: The Life, Nature and Cultivation of Anthroposophy*. Forest Row: Rudolf Steiner Press, 2011. [January 13-10 August, 1924]

GA 234; *Anthroposophy: An Introduction*. Trans. and intro. Owen Barfield. 2nd edition; London: Anthroposophical Publishing Co., 1961. [January 19-February 10, 1924][2]

Frederick Amrine, ed. GA 234; *Anthroposophy: An Introduction. Vol. 2: Supplemental Materials*. ([Amazon:]) Keryx, 2019.

Frederick Amrine. GA 234; *Anthroposophy: An Introduction. Vol. 3: Commentary*. ([Amazon:]) Keryx, 2020.

GA 235-240; *Karmic Relationships*. Lectures 1-82. Ed. and trans. Frederick Amrine. [Amazon:] Keryx, 2018-2020. [January 25-September 28, 1924].

---

[1] This title is out of print, but available in the Rudolf Steiner Archive at the url: https://www.rsarchive.org/GA/index.php?ga=GA0233. Lectures VIII and IX of this cycle are included in GA 260.

[2] This title is out of print, but available in the Rudolf Steiner Archive at the url: https://www.rsarchive.org/GA/index.php?ga=GA0234.

GA 270; *The First Class: Lessons and Mantras: The Michael School: Meditative Path in Nineteen Steps*. Ed. T. H. Meyer. Great Barrington: SteinerBooks, 2017. [February 15-August 2. 1924]

26; *Anthroposophical Leading Thoughts: The Cognitional Path of Anthroposophy – The Mystery of Michael*. Vols. 1-7. Ed. and trans. Frederick Amrine. ([Amazon:]) Keryx, 2019.

GA 270; *The First Class: Recapitulation Lessons and Mantras*. Ed. T. H. Meyer. Great Barrington: SteinerBooks, 2017. [April 3-Sept 20, 1924]

GA 308; *The Methodology of Waldorf Education*. Trans. Frederick Amrine. Keryx, 2019. [Stuttgart; April 8-11, 1924]

GA 309; *The Roots of Education*. Foundations of Waldorf Education XIX. Trans. Helen Fox and Frederick Amrine. [Bern; April 13-17, 1924]
https://www.waldorflibrary.org/books/3/view/52/ebooks/112/the-roots-of-education-ebook

GA 311; *The Art of Education*. Trans. Frederick Amrine. Keryx, 2019. [Torquay; August 12-20, 1924]

GA 243 [excerpts]; *True and False Paths in Spiritual Investigation*. Ed. and trans. Frederick Amrine. ([Amazon:]) Keryx, 2020. [August 14-22, 1924]

Introduction

Anthroposophy: An Introduction is one of Steiner's most important lecture cycles. In it, Steiner begins anew in light of the Christmas Conference, presenting anthroposophy in a language and approach that is fresh, concrete, and even more esoteric. He refers to his early book *Theosophy* in particular, saying that now he wants to recast that content in a less schematic, more inward fashion.

Given the obvious centrality of such a work to anthroposophy, it is astonishing that the cycle has remained out of print for a very long time. The present volume is part of a multi-pronged attempt to make it accessible again. It contains suggested emendations of the two versions available, plus notes, which are not included with the extant translations at all. It was also possible to reproduce for the first time the color plates, which are not available even in the German original.

Fortunately, the extant translation proper, in which Owen Barfield had a hand, is excellent. Its language is crisp and precise, as one would expect from a master of English prose style. It is also very British, and it is in places more highbrow than the original. But these are reasons to appreciate, rather than to denigrate the translation.

Thus I have decided not to retranslate the piece, even though the print edition can be hard to procure. For those who cannot obtain a printed copy, the same translation is available from the Rudolf Steiner Archive at:

https://www.rsarchive.org/GA/index.php?ga=GA0234.

Going over the latter version, I found various typos. These are listed below, together with emendations that bring it into conformity with the print edition.

The extant translation is in some regards dated, especially in its gendered language: for example, it consistently gives "man" for *der*

Mensch. I have not suggested emendations of the gendered language, however, because there are so many instances of it. The reader will kindly make the changes mentally as he or she reads.

The heart of the present volume is the full set of notes. Certain more extensive topics have been relegated either to appendices here, or to the commentary, which will be forthcoming in a separate volume at some future date, perhaps in 2020.

The online version of the translation does not include Owen Barfield's introduction, which I include in an appendix for those who have not been able to obtain a printed copy of the cycle.

Emendations to *The Rudolf Steiner Archive*'s Version

Page numbers refer to the print edition.

Emendations are indicated in **boldface** type.

Lecture 1

January 19, 1924

p. 20   Here is the sharp boundary between **man** and Nature.

p. 23   … Nature exists, that man can only approach her by letting her destroy him. [¶] Indeed, the men who lived thousands of years …

p. 17   In respect of all that is ***not*** man, there is – spiritual – …

p. 27   on the one hand, we have what the organism takes in; on the other, what it gives **off** – including even the physical body …

p. 28   At some past time the whole earth must have been in the condition in which **something** within man is today; …

p. 31   … I had with him ten or twenty years ago. In the **meantime** he may have been in Australia, or anywhere …

p. 34   Thus I release through my own activity something within this wide sea of ether that is similar to my own 'third man'. [¶] What is this that acts in the ether as a counter-image?

p. 35   I do not **find** there, as yet, what has been released …

p. 35   Going **backwards** in time is really no different …

p. 35   … the whole time-evolution is still there. **Whatever** was once there – and is of like nature …

Lecture 3

January 27, 1924

p. 40   It is for Anthroposophy to grasp man's part in the **supersensible** world.

p. 40   Man's being, however, reaches out into the **supersensible**. He carries his **supersensible** being from pre-earthly existence …

p. 40   There are, however, two gates which lead from the physical and etheric worlds to the **supersensible. …** when we realise that they are gates to the **supersensible** world …

p. 42   In this sense the moon is a gate to the **supersensible**, and one who studies it rightly …

p. 43   We cut our nails, for example, but **everything** within us is moving towards the surface …

p. 44   … not only the the indefinite feelings of love, to mention these once again, but **everything** in the subconscious depths of our souls …

p. 46   Even in childhood and early life we come into contact with people whose **relationship** to us remains external …

p. 48   That peculiar, intimate, inner relationship in which another person speaks from within us – as it were – indicates **ties** of destiny from the past.

p. 48   Thus the **ties** of destiny, which are usually felt only in the will …

Lecture 4

February 1, 1924

p. 53   But an indefinite impulse takes place in us, saying: I *will* this.

p. 55   … we look back on this interval of time, we do not find the ego *qua* experience. It was extinguished.

p. 57   We never get further in this way. We must begin by *experiencing* thinking. One does this …

p. 58   So, too, we strenuously endeavor, again and again, to **perform** the above activity …

p. 61   If you strengthen your thinking the super-terrestrial spatial world begins to concern you and the second man you have **discovered – just** as the earthly, physical world …

p. 62   … until one learns to distinguish the solid man from the fluid **man – this** inner surging and weaving element which really resembled a small ocean.

p. 68   This music is actually **performed**, but it remains unconscious; … I have referred to these things before, but it is my present intention to give a **résumé** of what has been developed …

p. 69   Only, we must be clear that there is a **considerable** difference between what we find in the world outside and what we find in man.

p. 73   … which streams in as living beings. **Indeed,** it is no merely general, abstract, astral weaving …

p. 77   This 'inspired' knowledge is attained by emptying our consciousness *after* strengthened thinking.

p. 77   And then we undergo what many who are striving for higher knowledge do not seek: we suffer what may be called the *pain of knowledge.*

p. 78   … with all our inwardness of heart and mind; that is, with our *soul forces.*

p. 80   And when you perceive a man clairvoyantly you are led to say: **He** is standing here and I see him …

p. 80   … the head of his last incarnation a little above the head of his present incarnation, and **somewhat** higher still, the head …

p. 81   He experiences a moral impulse and is expected to act in accordance with it, although he is compounded of all those **substances** which cannot do so. [Mistake in the original translation.]

p. 87   … its returning the air in this condition. **You feel** yourself entirely within the air …

p. 88   Only, to begin with, we feel what is here streaming towards us in the exhaled air; it is a *felt* outer world, that we have at first.

p. 91   … he perceives this or that or thinks about it. **He** has then a thought.

p. 95   One might compare theoretical anthroposophy to a **photograph**. If you are very anxious…

Lecture 7

February 8, 1924

p. 97   Or he is distressed in his dream by a frog approaching his hand; he takes hold of the frog and **finds** it soft.

p. 97   …. in the peculiar formations constituting the vault. If **we** pursue our studies further in this direction …

p. 98   He could have been in a **shipwreck**, or a friend may have proved unfaithful …

p. 100   We then **discover** the following intensely interesting fact.

p. 102   Nevertheless there is a strong resemblance between the **second**

p. 103   … it contracts and, instead of being something **all-embracing**, becomes smaller and smaller …

p. 104   Thus we gain the impression that imagination gives us **something** created by a great master-hand …

Lecture 8

February 9, 1924

p. 109   … rather than its detailed **content**. The individual content interests us less …

p. 109   It is the course of the **dream – just** that which does not …

p. 109   We see that, in a spiritual sense, the dream *is* the human being, as the seed is the plant.

p. 110   … in the plant-growth of the following year. [¶] It is just this way of studying …

p. 110   … the seed of a future life is being formed within the withering process that proceeds from man's *being* of a former life on earth.

p. 111   … with imaginative consciousness, we say to **ourselves**: Your keen intellect does not help you …

p. 112   And if we look at what man knows of himself while he dreams – dreams in his *sleep* – we have before us what man …

p. 118   I did this in my book *Theosophy*, where I followed more the accustomed line of thought of our age.

p. 118f.   … the whole spiritual aspect of our daily life, [¶] So we might put it this way.

Lecture 9

February 10, 1924

p. 123   … can return from death to birth. [¶] This is what we do in the spiritual world …

p. 127   We *are* now what we have experienced; we ***are*** our own spiritual worth corresponding thereto.

p. 124   … and then the individualities of higher spiritual beings. [¶] We live as spirit among human and non-human …

Page numbers refer to the print edition.

Emendations are indicated in **boldface** type.

Lecture 1

January 19, 1924

p. 19   My thought, however, flits past – a picture that **fluctuates, that** continually comes and goes, content to be merely a picture.

p. 19   What annihilates the thought again and again so that it must be kindled anew by our outer perception? **What is it that maintains the stone?** We say the stone 'exists': …

p. 20   Yet he has only **fluctuating** pictures – skimmed off, as it were, from the surfaces of things …

p. 21   And when he discovers that this surging, unreal life of his soul has something to do with that other world presented by nature, he is **perplexed by a fearsome riddle.**

p. 22   Thus, from two directions, **trying** questions confront man today.

p. 22   Figure 1:

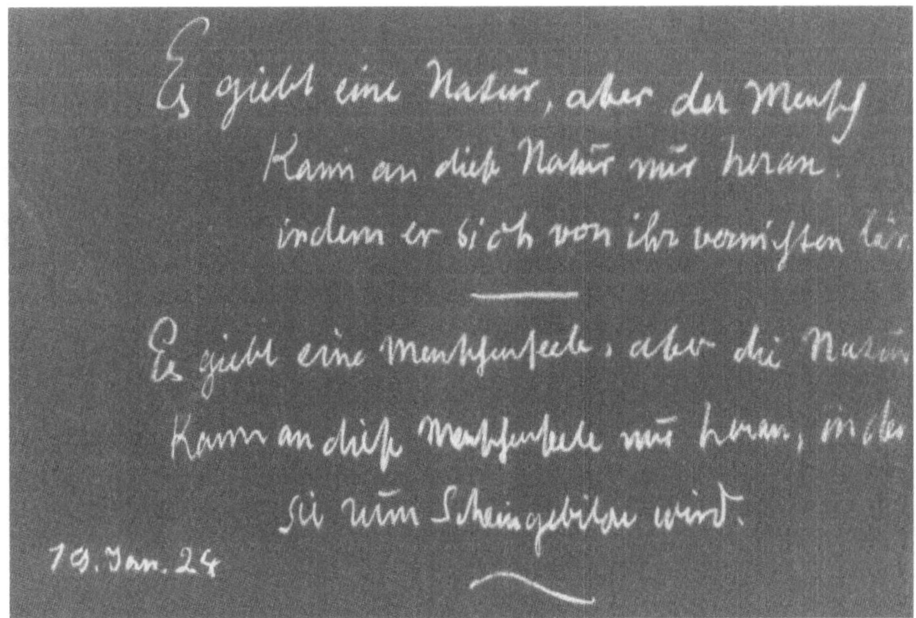

p. 22   These two truths live in the subconsciousness of man today. **And now man turns towards what lives, carried forward out of the primordial past into the present.** On the one hand, we have the …

Lecture 2

January 20, 1924

p. 27:   Insert **the following diagram** after this sentence: "It is what lies between these two stages that we must first discover."

p. 27   Insert **Fig. 2** after "It is what lies between these two stages that we must first discover":

Figure 2

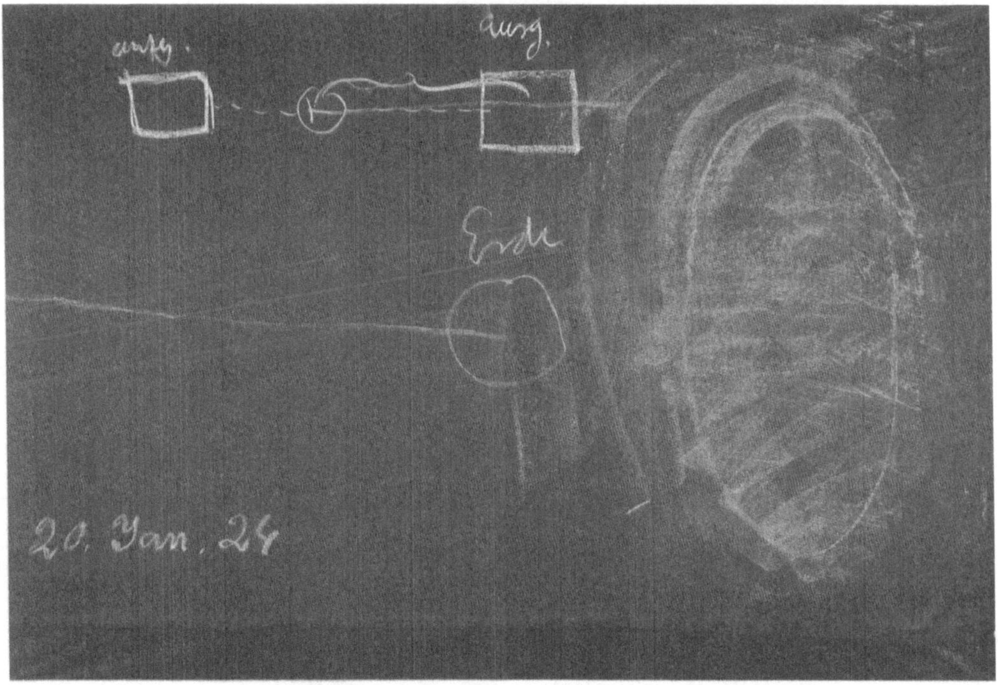

p. 27   Though external physical nature does destroy man's corpse, dissolving and dissipating it, man does, with his organism, **'pay back'** Nature.

p. 28   … you are led to trace it back to a similar condition in which it once was. **[See Fig. 2]** You have to say: …

p. 29   Let us contemplate, on the one hand, the long **period** of 25, 920 years.

p. 30   In doing so we pay special attention to the **inner force that drives out these representations.** In this way one comes to feel …

p. 30   I allow something to happen to me: I let Nature **stuff me** with thoughts. But I will no longer let myself be **stuffed** with thoughts, I will place …

p. 31   When we have so strengthened ourselves within that our thinking **feels only like the inner muscular power,** we are at once confronted …

p. 31   Let us say it is a crystal of salt or of quartz. **I look with this inner strengthening at a stone.** It seems to me like meeting a man: **Have I seen him already?** I am reminded of experiences …

p. 32   So we may say that, if a man takes trouble to develop such thinking he perceives, besides the physical, the etheric in himself, in plants, **in looking at the minerals, in memory of primordial times, that awaken the minerals.**

Now, what do we learn …

p. 32   When I simply lift this piece of chalk, I observe all sorts of things happening in the ether. **Oh,** lifting a piece of chalk is a complicated process. **My arm and my hand lift up the chalk. What my hand does, that is the development of a certain form in me. This** force **is present** in me in the waking state, not when I am asleep. If I follow what the ether does in transmuting food-stuffs **as we described**, I find this going on during both waking and sleeping states.

p. 33   … but in the way the third man acts. **(See Fig. 2)**

Thus I may say: …

p. 34   Thus I **unchain** through my own activity something within this wide sea of ether that is similar to my own 'third man'.

Now when I ask myself: What is it that I am unchaining? What is this that acts in the ether **otherwise** as the counter-image? … It is really an astral picture, **but it is** a mere *picture*.

p. 35   Insert Fig. 3 after the sentence ending: "… if I learn to apply to cosmic evolution what is briefly recapitulated in the way I described – I discover the following:"

Figure 3

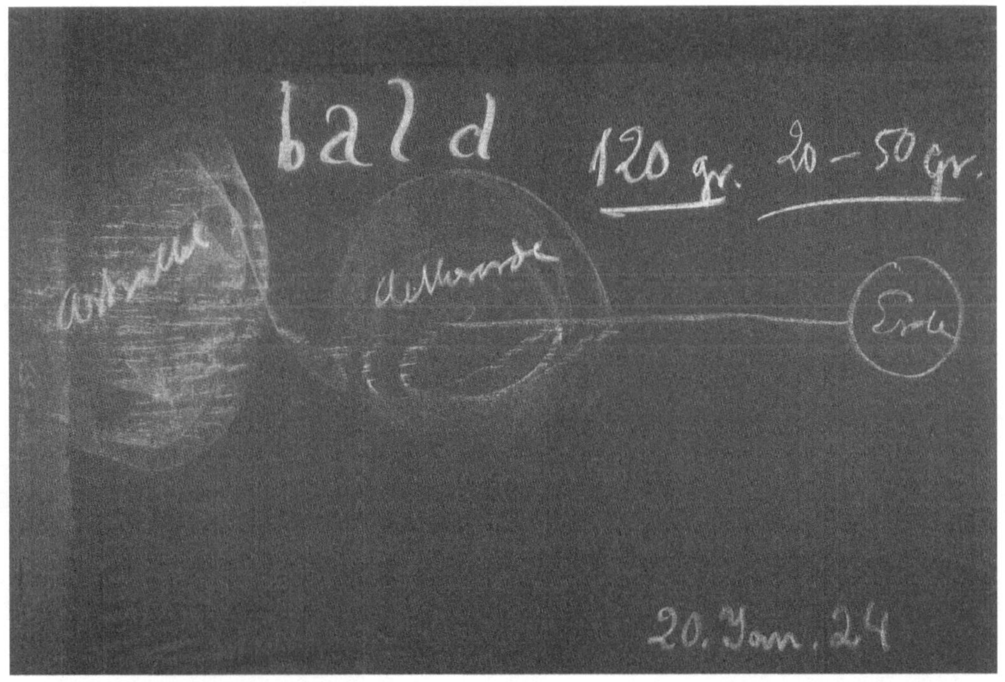

p. 35   It is over there, but shines as far as here; it sends images to us here. **(See Fig. 3) Here I have in place of space only time.** That which is of like nature with my own astral body was there in primeval times.

p. 36   **But** we understand, too, why cosmic riddles present themselves to him.

p. 36   You cannot really understand why there is here a form like this: 'b', then 'a', then 'l', then 'd', i.e. *bald* [soon]. **(See Fig. 3).** What are these forms doing side by side?

p. 37   At that time it was 'science' that one would become ill – under-nourished – if one did not get these one hundred and twenty grammes of protein. **[See Fig. 3]**

Lecture 3

January 27, 1924

p. 42   The configuration of the moon is, in fact, like that of the earth before it became quite mineral. [¶] **I am indicating that aphoristically to you today.** I should have to read you a large number …

p. 44   It is the beings themselves who sustain the moon, **that is, the psycho-spiritual element in it,** just as it is the psycho-spiritual in you that maintains your body. **And only if we know that** the physical moon once went out into cosmic space! But what went out is continually changing its substance …

p. 44   From this we free ourselves **from the lunar existence** in all that constitutes our present life. We are continually **tearing ourselves free from lunar existence**. When we hear or see outer things …

p. 45   … who came together when one was, perhaps, thirty years of age and the other twenty-five.

Figure 4

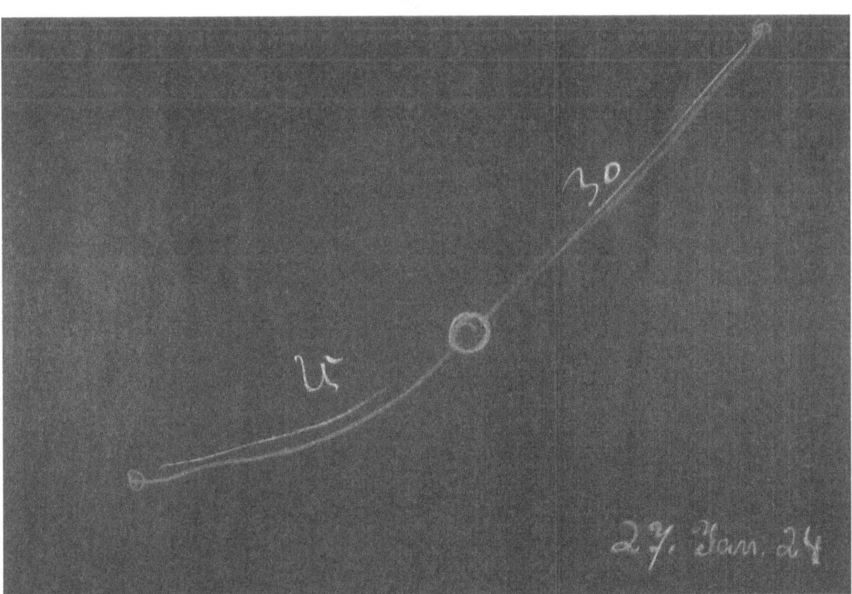

He will see in what a wonderful and extraordinary way …

p. 48   As I have said, I only want today to sketch these things in **an aphoristic** way in order to show you the path …

p. 48   That peculiar, intimate, inner **emergence** in which another person speaks from within **us indicates** ties of destiny from the past.

Lecture 4

February 1, 1924

p. 52   … and go through life with this perception, you encounter that **tragically** disturbing fact which intrudes on all human experience and of which I spoke.

p. 53   But there is another side, and this introduces us again – in a certain sense – to what is **tragic**.

p. 54   It contains **a tinge** man must value above all else in his life, for his whole manhood – his human dignity – depends on this. I refer to the moral **tinge**.

p. 54   They have to be experienced entirely within the soul; there, too, we must be able to **follow** them.

p. 54   … to obey moral principles which are not forced upon us. **As long as we have to say: What our drives, instincts, passions, emotion etc. force upon us, is within us – fine; we must perform this or that deed.** Yet man cannot become an 'abstract' being only obeying *laws*.

p. 54   … yet are bound up with what is most valuable in us – the moral **tinge.**

p. 55   But it is **really** necessary that what becomes a riddle of life for a man be clearly recognized as such? If people had to live by what they are clear about they would soon die. It is really the contributions to the general mood **of life** from unclear, subconscious depths that compose the main stream of our life. We should say that he alone feels the riddles of life who can formulate them in an intellectually clear way and **bring them** before us **on a tray**: first riddle, second riddle, etc. Indeed, such people are the shallowest. **What moves deep within us are the riddles of life that are experienced.**

p. 56   For the spiritual always reveals itself as something that **flares** up and dies down …

p. 57   Today we will only **place** this path **before your souls** in bare outline, for we intend to give the **sketch** of a whole anthroposophical structure **in an entirely elementary way.** We will begin again …

p. 59   The main thing is that the moment you feel this second man within you, supra-terrestrial things begin to concern you in the way only terrestrial things did before. **I mean the spatially supra-terrestrial things.** In this moment, when you feel your thought take on an inner life …

p. 59   After you have intensified your thinking and come to feel the second man within, **then the moment begins when you become especially interested in this second man, but** your earthly environment begins to interest you less than **before. One** does not become a dreamer …

p. 59   One does not become a visionary and say: Oh! I have learnt to know the spiritual world; the earthly is **insubstantial** and of less value.

p. 61   It is a most significant leap in consciousness that one takes here – a complete metamorphosis **of consciousness.** From this point …

p. 62   … and now induces a kind of 'touching' within me – a touching that also **lives** in an organism; …

p. 62   … we see, in sharp contours, liver, spleen, kidney, lung, bones, muscles and nerve strands. **[Fig. 5]** These can be drawn; …

p. 63   … it is a great drop. **[Fig. 5]** Wherever water is free to take its own form, it takes that of a drop.

p. 63   Every drop, whether small or large, appears as a reflection of the universe itself. **[Fig. 5]** Whether you take a drop of rain, or the waters of earth as a whole …

p. 64   … the second whom we **come to feel** within ourselves in our strengthened thinking as the human etheric body.

p. 64   This means, that we are developing a great inner **impulsivity**. Now, as you know, one can …

p. 65   For now, on exposing one's empty consciousness to the indefinite on all sides, the spiritual world proper **forces its way in**. One says: …

p. 65   … of the cosmos when you traverse the path I have described.

Figure 5

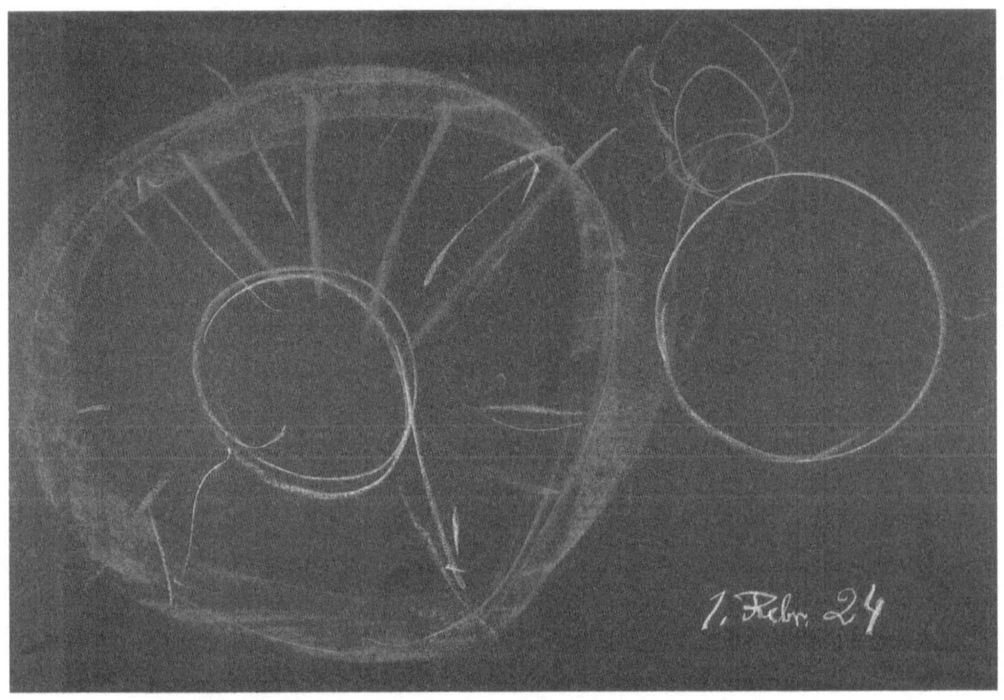

[¶] A third thing is now added to the former metamorphosis …

p. 65   I ask you to notice that I am talking of the world of **ostensibility**; we shall see in the next few days …

p. 66   Now we can go **further. We** now say to ourselves: …

p. 66   He gradually learns to know the spiritual **with which man is tinged** in respiration. He learns to say to himself **in knowing**: You have a physical body; …

p. 66   Man's fluid organization with its regular but ever changing life will never be grasped by ordinary thinking. **Fluid man** can only be grasped …

p. 67   … and which can only be apprehended in images (Bilder) – in moving, **sculptural** images.

February 2, 1924

p. 70   I pointed out that, from out of the etheric everything, whether it be a large or small drop, is made spherical. **[He draws Fig. 6]**

Figure 6

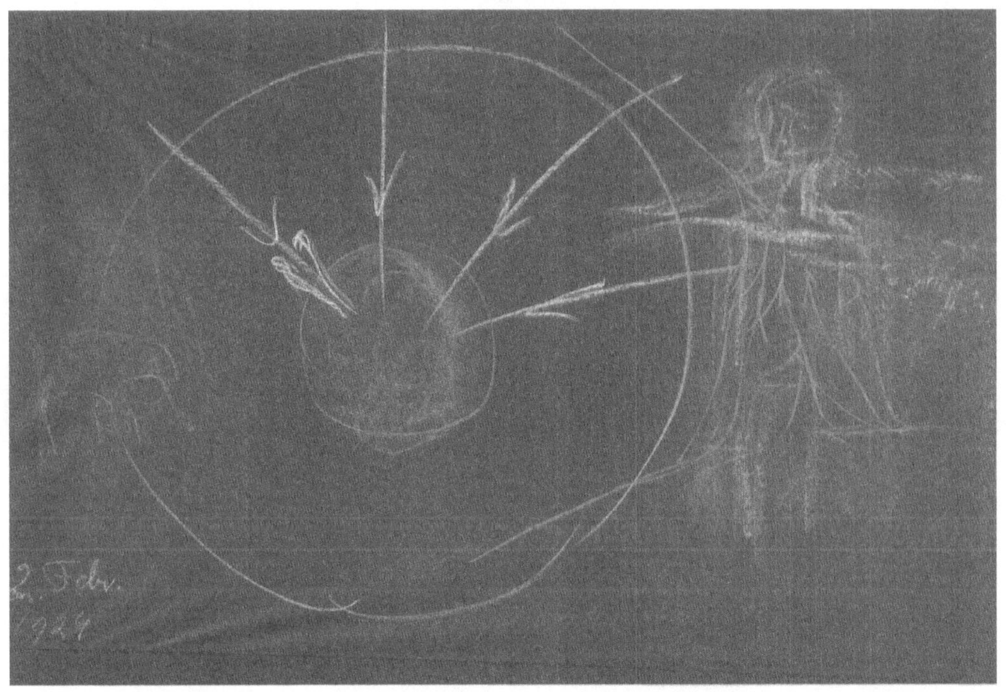

p. 70   In its present form the human etheric body is closely moulded to the **human** physical body. ... which otherwise conforms to the human shape, only protrudes a little beyond the arm, whereas below it is widely extended. **[Fig. 6, right]** But **this etheric body** has from the cosmos the tendency to take on spherical form

p. 71   … and one really perceives it in the way I described yesterday, i.e. as an inner musical element, a **vortical**, weaving life … it is transformed into the human astral form, whereby complicated things appear. **[He draws.]**

p. 71   One might say, the human being **compels** his astral body by subduing the centripetal astral forces.

p. 72   He was bathing one day and noticed, on lifting his leg out of the water, how much heavier it was than when in the water, and exclaimed: **I have found it!** Eureka! I have found **it!** ... Thus, if you think of Archimedes in his bath, here his physical leg **[he draws]** and here the same leg formed of water …

p. 73   … one finds the etheric at work in all the **watery weaving** of the earth.

p. 74   It is just as when you look down an avenue and see the trees drawing closer and closer together on account of perspective; you see the whole avenue **according to space**.

p. 74   Let us assume we are observing the astral body of a person on the 2nd February 1924. Let this be the person. **[He draws, Fig. 6, right]** He does …

p. 75   But imagine some being or other were here **[Fig. 6, right, underneath]**, and by means of cords mechanically connected …

p. 77   … in which we perceive the beings that express themselves through these images – hear a kind of music of the spheres, **but something substantial.**

p. 78   We can then experience the above identification with, and coming to life in, another being **entirely**. Only then do we learn the **exponentially** highest degree of love …

p. 78   But nothing remains of all that made up that physical body; it has been absorbed into the elements. **Nothing is left of it.** Your innermost being of that time …

p. 79   And, in addition, you have a surging organism of warmth, **something organic that is warm and cold**. In this you yourself live.

p. 80   In fact, the more this consciousness is developed, the more clearly do we see, in a kind of perspective **[he draws]**, the head of his last incarnation …

p. 85   We deprive the outer air of its life-giving power and return, not a vitalizing, but a **deadening** element. … we breathe in the vitalizing and breathe out the **deadening** element.

p. 85   I should now like to describe this in quite a **popular** way.

p. 87   Of course, it is a spiritual **process**, not a **process of breathing**; you receive the *impression* made by your exhaled air. **But it is not only that**. In this exhaled air … There is my body and it is breathing out this **deadening** air.

p. 87   You now know that man's astral body, when within the physical, delights in the inhaled air **(if I might express myself thus)**, using it unconsciously …

Figure 8

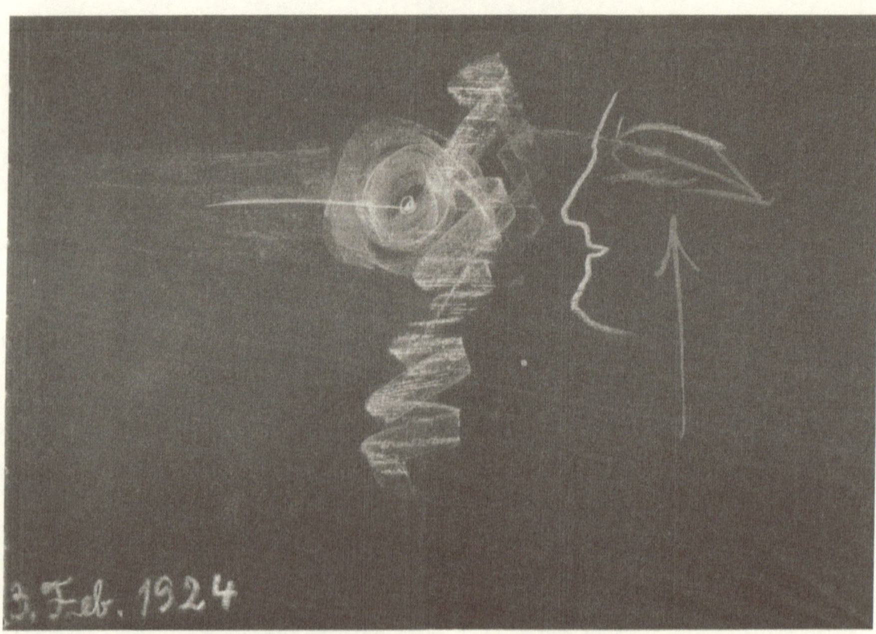

p. 87   Only in 'inspiration' does this become conscious. **[Fig. 8, left]** Further, we receive a striking impression. It is as if what confronts the sleeping man **[he draws]** stood out against a dark background. … We recognize its essential nature, inasmuch as our everyday thoughts now leave us and the active, cosmic thoughts – the objective, **reigning** thoughts of the world **that are creative** – appear before us in what is flowing out of ourselves.

Figure 9

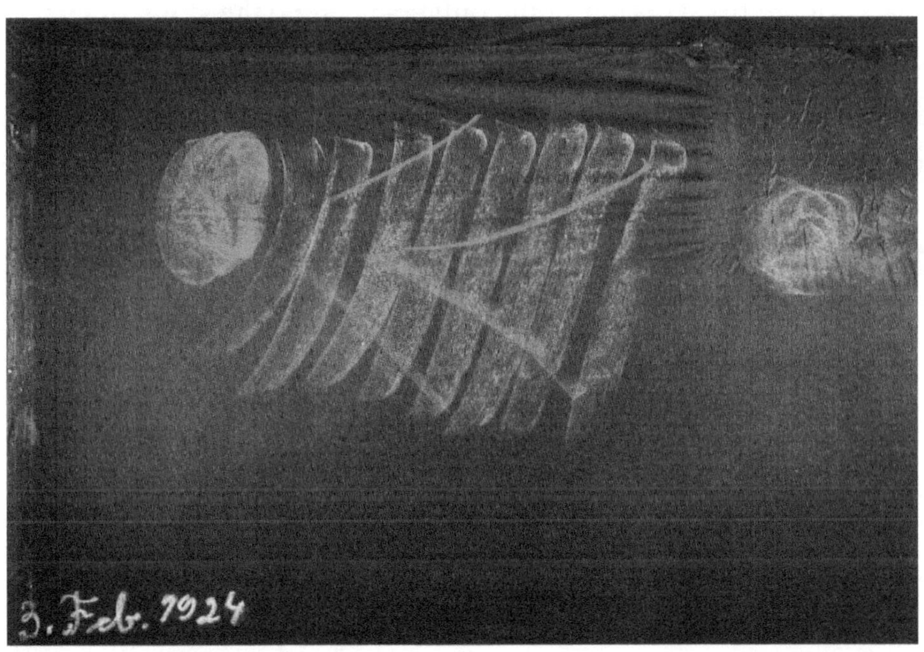

p. 89   … when they are awakened, man, through them, beholds himself from without. Let us see what this really means. **[Figs. 8 & 9]**

p. 90   Our concept of time must undergo a complete **conceptual metamorphosis**. … or has returned to his former lives on earth. When talking **popularly** we say: he is 'outside' his body.

p. 91   In one case – representing it schematically**[see figure on p. 92]** – you have man's environment …

p. 91   It really is as follows: **We perceive conceptually.** Our perceptions enter our body, whereas our thought **only** 'stands out.'

p. 92   … just as we form a thought of the outer world. The thought is always **present**.

p. 92   Just think how many people find it helps to repeat a thing aloud; others make curious gestures when they want to **imbue their minds with something.**

p. 94   We see the working of the universe behind the **stage** of our existence.

p. 94   If it were to remain a mere thought, we would have to be creatures of **papier-mâché**, not men living … as apathetic towards such things as if they really we made of **papier-mâché.** Civilised people today often appear to be such **figures made of papier-mâché.**

p. 95   This becomes for him a **cosmic** riddle. But now, as a result …

Lecture 7

February 8, 1924

p. 98   There is a cave-like opening and into this the sun is still shining. **He goes inside, dreaming.** It soon begins to grow dark, …

p. 99   The second kind of dream, however, **conjured for** him and pictures, although in transformed pictures, **basically his whole organism.**

p. 101   … that he then advances beyond the ordinary more or less empty, abstract thinking to it thinking **that is inwardly concrete**, pictorial …

p. 102   Look at this sketch I have drawn **[Fig. 10]**. It has an inner configuration and includes the most varied forms.

Figure 10

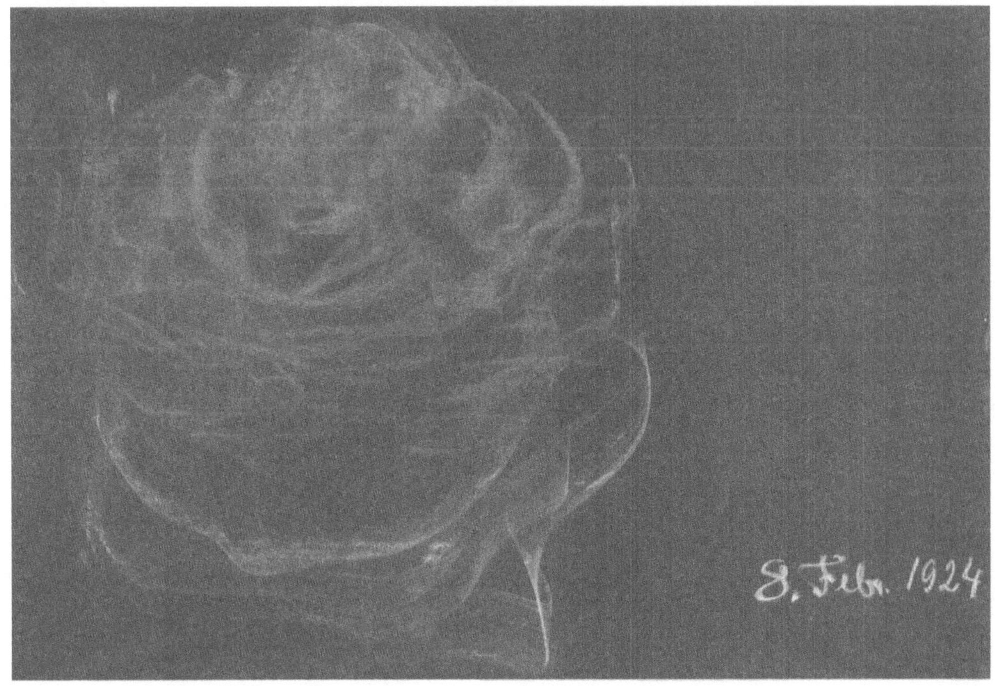

p. 105   But if we seek to grasp still deeper phenomena of life, the riddles to which I referred become **even more burning**. Those who have been here some time …

p. 105   At last, as his consciousness began to function again, he found himself in a **homeless shelter** in Berlin …

p. 106   To take dreams seriously – especially in regard to their *intentions* (not *wishes*) – is the **flip-side** of this condition of obliterated consciousness.

pp. 106-107   For a knowledge of the human being the dream-life of such a **pathological** patient **as I have depicted it** is really much more interesting than the dream-life **let us not say of a Philistine, but rather of** an ordinary contemporary.

p. 107   … nevertheless the caricature has the inherent possibility of growing into a perfect organ. **We say to ourselves, when we contemplate the caricature, that is something that could grow into a perfect organ.** This leads to the studies we shall be pursuing tomorrow. They **are rooted** in the question: …

p. 107   You see, moreover, that we must really look more deeply into the life of man then we usually find **comfortable**; otherwise we shall find no point …

p. 109   … If a man has no sense of ordinary realities, no interest in ordinary realities, no interest in the details of others' lives, if he is so 'superior' **(I say that in quotes)** that he sails through life without troubling about its details, **that alone is a sign that** he is not a genuine seer.

p. 111   The rhythmic organization contained in the **chest-cavity** is the connecting link between them …

p. 113   One might **say: If** this be man **[he draws Fig. 11],** and this the memory within him. Imagination at once …

Figure 11

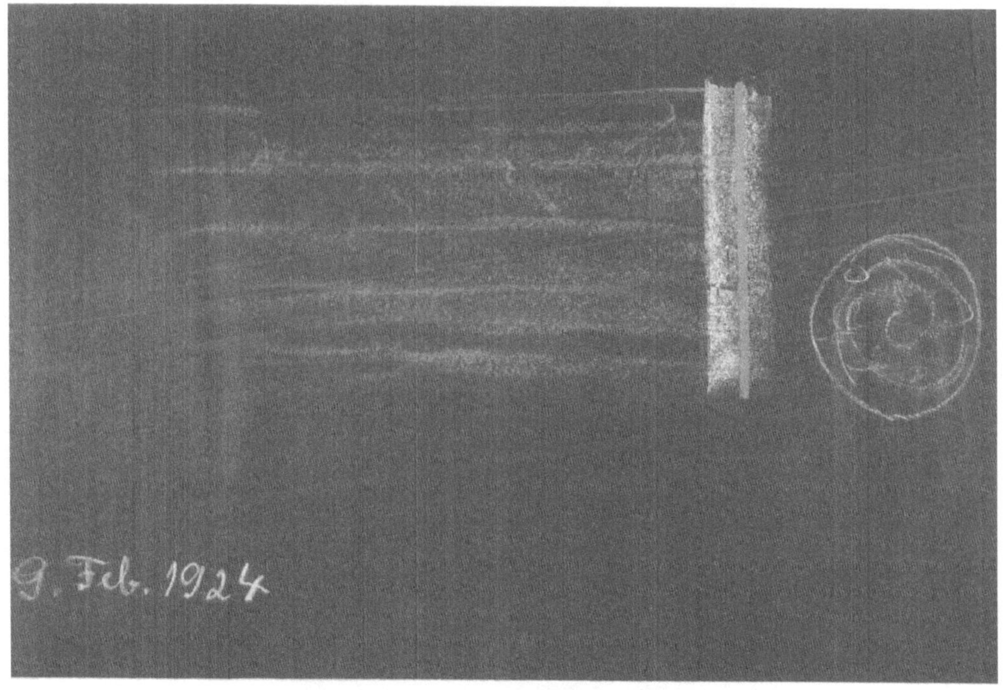

p. 113   In ordinary consciousness memory is confined, as it were, to a single **moment. Memory is expanded in time, when we have it before the imaginative consciousness.** Indeed, it is really …

p. 113   This is how we gaze into the tableau and know that the memory we bear within us in ordinary consciousness is a **very bad** illusion.

p. 113   All that is past becomes present; it is there, though **perspectivally removed.**

p. 113   This lasts some days and is his **obvious and** natural life-element.

p. 117   And then we go farther back, experiencing our life again, but backwards. **We know that during this time when we experience our lives again retrospectively, we experience the meaning of our life for the world. During this time we are bound to the earth, for it is only the other side of the earthly deeds that we experience.**

p. 117   We experience it now with a very **sharply** divided consciousness

p. 123   These conceal, to a certain extent, what we have inscribed into the world through our deeds, thoughts and feelings. **[Fig. 12]**

Figure 12

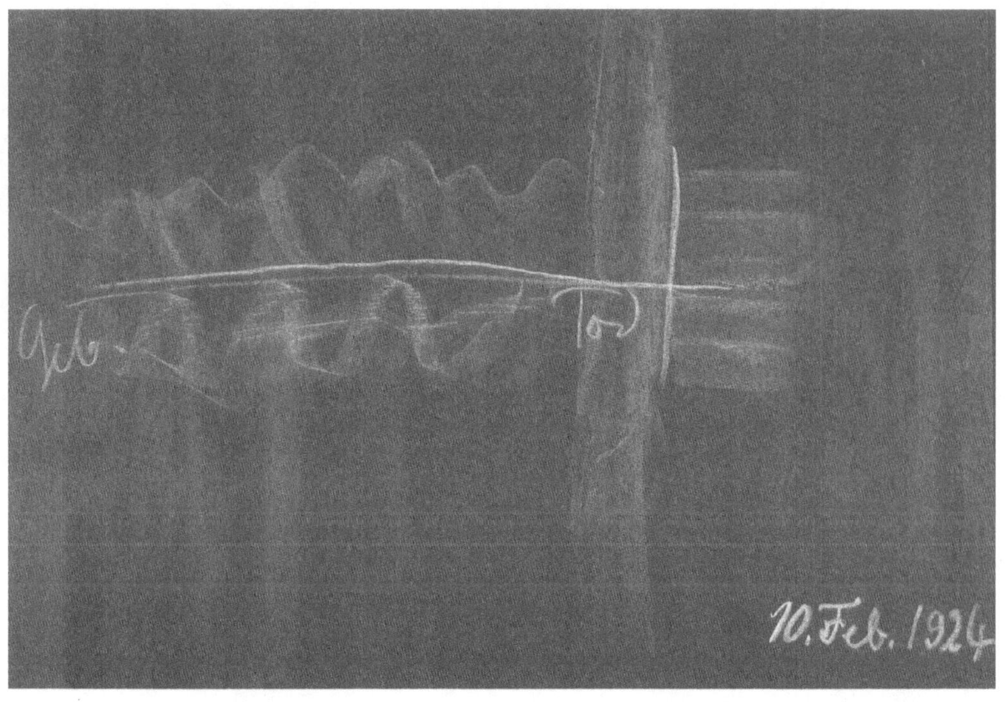

p. 128   … to use yesterday's metaphor – permeating these experiences during to retrospective part of the life between death and **birth. We** now stand face to face …

Notes

The full German title translates literally: *Anthroposophy: A Summary after Twenty-One Years: Simultaneously Guidance in Presenting it to the World.*

Lecture 1

January 19, 1924

p. 13: If you have not this feeling and think you can simply present the subject in an absolute sense – as one might have done twenty years ago – you will find yourselves more and more presenting Anthroposophy in a false light. Our Christmas meeting should mark a beginning in the opposite direction ...

The Christmas Conference took place in Dornach from December 24, 1923 to January 1, 1924. It was a refounding of the Society on a more esoteric basis. The central event was Rudolf Steiner's recitation of the Foundation Stone meditation, laying it in the hearts of the membership. Rudolf Steiner also assumed leadership of the Society, which he had studiously avoided up to that point. See CW 260: *The Christmas Conference for the Foundation of the General Anthroposophical Society 1923/1924: The Laying of the Foundation Stone: Lectures and Addresses: Discussion of the Statutes: Dornach, 24 December 1923 to 1 January 1924* (Hudson, NY: Anthroposophic Press, 1990).

*

p. 15: Yet this Realm of Nature cannot suffer the human form within her own system of laws. / *This sentence and the rest of the paragraph in which it occurs must of course be read in the context of the lecture as a whole. Taken by itself it may well arouse the objection: 'The human form is as much within Nature's system of laws as those of the plants and animals. Certainly Nature destroys it after death; but does she not also bring it to birth?' It may help to remind the reader that Dr. Steiner at this stage merely putting into words a feeling, which, he expressly says, arises when we stand in the presence of death. Later on in the book, when he deals with the relation in which the human body stands to the world of nature, he shows how the human form in fact has an origin quite different from those of other living creatures." [Owen Barfield]*

The key word is *"this* [Realm of Nature]." Steiner means Nature as not overridden by higher human forces, which intervene to counteract her otherwise destructive tendencies.

*

p. 22: But modern consciousness has discarded this ancient knowledge.

See Owen Barfield's magisterial study *Saving the Appearances: A Study in Idolatry* (London: Faber, 1957; rpt. 2nd edn. Middletown, CT: Wesleyan UP, 1988), in which he argues that "original participation" as a human consciousness of divine wisdom shining from *behind* the phenomena and passively apprehended, was gradually rooted out by "alpha thinking," resulting eventually in the "onlooker consciousness" that arose first in the Renaissance.

*

p. 23: ... for he can no longer realise what Raphael could still conjure ...

Raffaello Sanzio da Urbino (1483-1520), known by his first name in English, Raffael, "was an Italian painter and architect of the High Renaissance. His work is admired for its clarity of form, ease of composition, and visual achievement of the Neoplatonic ideal of human grandeur." [*Wikipedia*].

*

p. 23: They looked at the corpse passing over into external Nature as into a vast Moloch, and saw it destroyed.

"Moloch" (alternatively "Molech") was the name in the Tanakh or Old Testament of a Caananite god associated with child sacrifice, hence all-devouring.

47

Lecture 2

January 20, 1924

The title of this lecture translates literally as "Meditative Consciousness."

*

> *p. 27: We speak so glibly of the blood man bears within him; but has anyone ever investigated the blood within the living human organism itself?*

Cf. Owen Barfield, *Saving the Appearances*, ch. XII, "Some Changes," where he offers a fascinating meditation on "unshed" (i.e., participated) blood and "shed" (i.e., unparticipated) blood. The former is unconsciously merged with our selves, while the latter has become an object, apart from us.

*

> *p. 29: Now, you can look at the vernal point of the zodiac, where the sun rises every spring. This point is not stationary; it is advancing.*

See Rudolf Steiner, *Interdisciplinary Astronomy*, 4 vols. ([Amazon:] Keryx, 2019).

*

> *p. 29: Through long periods the earth consisted of substances like those within us at a certain stage of digestion – the stage midway between ingestion and egestion, when the former passes over into the latter.*

"Egestion" is a technical term that means "the act or process of discharging undigested or waste material from a cell or organism, specifically: defecation."

*

> *p. 29: But this earth must once have been in a condition in which it was subjected to outer laws.*

See especially Chapter 4 of Rudolf Steiner, CW 13; *An Outline of Esoteric Science*, trans. Catherine E. Creeger (Great Barrington, MA: SteinerBooks, 1997). An otherwise excellent earlier translation by George Adams bore the unfortunate title *Occult Science*. At the time of writing, Steiner was the head of the Theosophical Society in Germany, and the word *Geheimwissenschaft* in his title was meant to echo Blavatsky's tome, *The Secret Doctrine*. GA 13 is now considered one of the four "basic books" of anthroposophy.

*

> *p. 30: We are accustomed merely to allow the 'ideas' or, mental presentations [Vorstellungen], whereby we perceive the world, to arise within us – merely to represent the outer world to ourselves with the help of such ideas.*

See Appendix 2.

*

> *p. 30: And for the last few centuries man has become so accustomed to copy merely the outer world in his ideas, that he does not realise his power of also forming ideas freely from within. To do this is to meditate; it is to fill one's consciousness with ideas not derived from external Nature, but called up from within.*

This is the main idea conveyed in Rudolf Steiner's *Philosophy of Freedom* (see *The Essential Philosophy of Freedom*, edited and translated by Frederick Amrine, Keryx, 2017). Steiner has neatly conjoined the main idea of this "basic book" with that of another, *How to Know Higher Worlds*. For more on this important conjunction, see the Commentary.

*

> *p. 30: Through meditation, however, it is possible to strengthen our power of thinking ... stretching out an arm.*

Cf. the phenomenological concept of "intentionality." According to this idea, all mental phenomena have an implied referent. Intentionality is a fundamental mental faculty, and can be strengthened through training.

Although he antedated phenomenology by a century, Goethe's scientific work depends crucially upon just such a "metamorphosis of the scientist."

*

> *p. 31: At length we notice that this thinking activity is a 'tension', a 'touching', an inner experience, like the experience of our own muscular force.*

Cf. Plato's description of perception as a kind of higher "touching." Remembering that Plato experienced the ideas as something outside that can be *perceived* – the etymology of "idea" is the past participle of the verb "to see" – this description ceases to be paradoxical.

*

> *p. 31: Thus I am led to speak, with some justification, of an "etheric body" as well as the physical. ... then the third man, which I will call the 'astral' man (red).*

See Appendix 3.

*

> *p. 35: Going backwards in time is really no different from seeing a distant object ... Fundamentally speaking, the whole time-evolution is still there. .... Here I touch on something that, spiritually, is actively present and makes time into space.*

See the Commentary on this important idea.

*

> *p. 36: The way of regarding things that I have put before you is really learning to read in the world and in man. By "learning to read" we become gradually near to the solution of our riddles.*

Cf. the traditional concept of "reading in the book of nature." "The Book of Nature is a religious and philosophical concept originating in the Latin Middle Ages which views nature as a book to be read for knowledge and understanding. ... Early theologians believed the Book of Nature was a source of God's revelation to mankind: when read alongside sacred scripture, the 'book' of nature and the study of God's creations would lead to a knowledge of God himself. The concept corresponds to the early Greek philosophical belief that man, as part of a coherent universe, is capable of understanding the design of the natural world through reason. The concept is frequently deployed by philosophers, theologians, and scholars. The first use of the phrase is unknown. However, Galileo used the phrase, quoting Tertullian, when he wrote of how 'We conclude that God is known first through Nature, and then again, more particularly, by doctrine; by Nature in His works, and by doctrine in His revealed word'." [*Wikipedia*]

Lecture 3

January 27, 1924

p. 39: In this connection we must bear in mind what I have already explained in the News Sheet for Members *when describing the Free College of Spiritual Science ...*

"At the heart of the Anthroposophical Society is the [Free College of Spiritual Science], an institution intended to be an esoteric school for spiritual scientific research and study. During the course of 1924 Rudolf Steiner held 19 esoteric lessons in which he introduced his followers to a series of meditations (mantras) along with instructions and guidelines for their use. This set of lessons is known as the First Class and they are made available to those who become members of the School." (*Anthroposophical Society in America*)

*

p. 40: He carries his supersensible being from pre-earthly existence into the earthly realm, and carries it out again at death – out of the physical and etheric too.

See the elegant chapter of *Esoteric Science* entitled "Sleep and Death," which is one of the best introductions to anthroposophy generally. (CW 13; *An Outline of Esoteric Science*, trans. Catherine E. Creeger [Great Barrington, MA: SteinerBooks, 1997]).

*

p. 40: There are, however, two gates which lead from the physical and etheric worlds to the supersensible. One is the moon, the other the sun.

This concept forms the opening of Steiner's magnificent, 82-lecture exploration of karma, which is known in English as *Karmic Relationships*. See my new translation, Rudolf Steiner, *Karmic Relationships 1-3: Archetypal Karmic Phenomena* ([Amazon:] Keryx, 2018).

*

p. 41: And whoever studies, for example, the Vedas of India or the Yoga philosophy from this point of view, will feel deep reverence for what he finds.

The Vedas are a collection of hymns written in Sanskrit as part of the Vedic religion in the Northwest of India sometime during approximately 1,500 and 1,200 BCE. They are the oldest layer of both Sanskrit and the Hindu religion. These hymns formed a liturgical body that in part grew up around the soma ritual and sacrifice, and were recited or chanted during rituals. (Soma seems to have been some kind of hallucinogenic drink.) The most important collection is the Rigveda.

Yoga (which means "yolking" or "union") is one of the six major orthodox schools of Hinduism. Its basic text is the *Yoga-sutra*s by Patanjali (dates unknown). "Yoga holds with Samkhya that the achievement of spiritual liberation (*moksha*) occurs when the spirit (*purusha*) is freed from the bondage of matter (*prakriti*) that has resulted from ignorance and illusion." [*Britannica*]

*

pp. 45-46: (Now we begin to understand people like Goethe's friend Knebel, whose experience of life was deep and varied and who said in his old age: On looking back on my life it seems as if every step had been so ordained that I had to arrive finally at a definite point.)

Karl Ludwig von Knebel (1744-1834). The quote is from *Knebels literarischer Nachlaß und Briefwechsel*, ed. Varnhagen von Ense and Mundt, 2nd edn., vol. III, p. 452.

*

p. 48: One experiences this in an essentially different way, however, when one attains a certain stage of the path described in my book Knowledge of the Higher Worlds and Its Attainment, *or in the second part of my* Occult Science.

CW 10; *How to Know Higher Worlds: A Modern Path of Initiation*, trans. Christopher Bamford, Classics in Anthroposophy (Great Barrington, MA: Anthroposophic Press, 1994. On *Occult Science* (more recently published as *Esoteric Science*), see above.

*

p. 51: We shall now begin to describe the constitution of man somewhat differently from the way it is done in my Theosophy.

CW 9; *Theosophy* (1904; many English editions are available, including now a very inexpensive Kindle Edition from Amazon). This early work presents the basics of Steiner's spiritual psychology using the terminology of theosophy. A much more dynamic (but also much more difficult) account is to be found in the middle four lectures of Rudolf Steiner, *A Psychology of Body, Soul, & Spirit* (New York: SteinerBooks, 1999), which includes a valuable introduction by Robert Sardello.

Lecture 4

February 1, 1924

The title of this lecture translates literally as "Strengthened Thinking and the Second Man: The Weaving of Respiration and the Man of Air."

*

p. 54: The conflict and settlement must therefore take place entirely within the soul. ... The moral life does not begin until emotions, impulses, instincts, passions, outbursts of temperament, etc., are subordinated to the settlement, reached entirely within the soul, between moral laws grasped in a purely spiritual way and the soul itself.

This is surely an evocation of Friedrich Schiller (1759-1805), the dramatist who became one of Goethe's closest friends and collaborators. Schiller was also a lyric poet and a historian, but Rudolf Steiner, like several of Schiller's contemporaries, considered him a great philosopher above all. Steiner was influenced deeply by Schiller's essay *On the Aesthetic Education of Man in a Series of Letters* (1794), of which this passage is reminiscent. A magnificent English translation by Elizabeth M. Wilkinson and L. A. Willoughby, with facing German and extensive commentary, was published by Oxford UP in 1967 (rpt. in paperback since), and it has helped bring this neglected masterpiece some measure of the attention it deserves.

*

p. 55: The ego begins to think in St. Augustine, continues through Descartes, and attains a somewhat coquettish expression in Bergsonism today.

St. Augustine: Saint Augustine of Hippo (354-430) "was a Roman African, early Christian theologian and philosopher from Numidia whose writings influenced the development of Western Christianity and Western philosophy. He was the bishop of Hippo Regius in North Africa and is viewed as one of the most important Church Fathers in Western Christianity for his writings in the Patristic Era. Among his most

55

important works are *The City of God, On Christian Doctrine* and *Confessions*." [*Wikipedia*]

Descartes: "René Descartes (1596–1650) was a creative mathematician of the first order, an important scientific thinker, and an original metaphysician. During the course of his life, he was a mathematician first, a natural scientist or "natural philosopher" second, and a metaphysician third. In mathematics, he developed the techniques that made possible algebraic (or 'analytic') geometry. In natural philosophy, he can be credited with several specific achievements: co-framer of the sine law of refraction, developer of an important empirical account of the rainbow, and proposer of a naturalistic account of the formation of the earth and planets (a precursor to the nebular hypothesis). More importantly, he offered a new vision of the natural world that continues to shape our thought today: a world of matter possessing a few fundamental properties and interacting according to a few universal laws. This natural world included an immaterial mind that, in human beings, was directly related to the brain; in this way, Descartes formulated the modern version of the mind–body problem. In metaphysics, he provided arguments for the existence of God, to show that the essence of matter is extension, and that the essence of mind is thought. Descartes claimed early on to possess a special method, which was variously exhibited in mathematics, natural philosophy, and metaphysics, and which, in the latter part of his life, included, or was supplemented by, a method of doubt." [*Stanford Encyclopedia of Philosophy*]

Bergsonism: Henri Bergson (1859-1941) was a great and highly influential philosopher who prized intuition above rationality, and was awarded the Nobel Prize in Literature. Bergson attempted to defend the possibility of human free will by radically redefining the notions of time, causality and thinking. His most important publications were *Time and Free Will* (1889), *Matter and Memory* (1896), *Creative Evolution* (1907), and *The Two Sources of Morality and Religion* (1932). In *The Riddles of Philosophy* (1973; [Great Barrington, Massachusetts:] SteinerBooks, 2009) Steiner applauds Bergson's epistemology while lamenting the flimsiness of his vitalistic theories of evolution. Bergson was a serious philosopher: it is not clear what Steiner means by "a somewhat coquettish expression."

*

p. 62: Through such 'imaginative' thinking as I have described we come, at first, to feel this inward touching of the second man within us; we come, too, to see this in connection with the far spaces of the universal ether.

Steiner refers constantly to Imagination, Inspiration, and Intuition. The most systematic treatment is arguably GA 12; *The Stages of Higher Knowledge: Imagination, Inspiration, Intuition* (Great Barrington, MA: SteinerBooks, 2009). Like Wordsworth, Steiner saw Imagination as more than reason, "reason in its most exalted mood." A good way to understand Imagination, Inspiration, and Intuition is to recall, and then expand, Plato's Allegory of the Cave, in which everyday thoughts are revealed to be but the shadows of a higher, more active and intuitive thinking activity. Steiner followed the German Idealists and the Romantics in calling this mode of intuitive thinking Imagination. By the same token, Steiner argued that there are higher modes of cognition of which everyday feeling and willing are but the shadows of Inspiration and Intuition respectively.

*

p. 63: Take the whole fluid element of our earth – its water; it is a great drop. Wherever water is free to take its own form, it takes that of a drop. The fluid element tends everywhere to be drop-like.

On this and many other matters, see Theodor Schwenk's fabulous book *Sensitive Chaos: The Creation of Flowing Forms in Water and Air* (London: Rudolf Steiner Press, 1996).

*

p. 63: This music is actually performed, but it remains unconscious; only the upper rebound is in consciousness. This is the lyre of Apollo, the inner musical instrument that the instinctive, primeval wisdom still recognized in man. I have referred to these things before ...

See the lectures of September 9, 1908 in GA 106; *Egyptian Myths and Mysteries* (Hudson, New York: Anthroposophic Press, 1971); December 30, 1913 in GA 149; *Christ and the Spiritual World and the Search for the Holy Grail* (1963; Forest Row: Rudolf Steiner Press, 2008); and June 2, 1923 in GA 291; *Colour*, trans. by John Salter and Pauline Wehrle (Forest Row, East Sussex: Rudolf Steiner Press, 1992).

Lecture 5

February 2, 1924

p. 72: This loss of weight in fluid is an old piece of knowledge. You know, of course, that it has been ascribed to Archimedes.

Archimedes of Syracuse (c. 287-c. 212 BCE) was a Greek mathematician, inventor, and astronomer. He is certainly the greatest mathematician of antiquity, and one of the greatest ever. "Archimedes anticipated modern calculus and analysis by applying concepts of infinitesimals and the method of exhaustion to derive and rigorously prove a range of geometrical theorems, including the area of a circle, the surface area and volume of a sphere, and the area under a parabola. Other mathematical achievements include deriving an accurate approximation of pi, defining and investigating the spiral bearing his name, and creating a system using exponentiation for expressing very large numbers. He was also one of the first to apply mathematics to physical phenomena, founding hydrostatics and statics, including an explanation of the principle of the lever. He is credited with designing innovative machines, such as his screw pump, compound pulleys, and defensive war machines to protect his native Syracuse from invasion." [*Wikipedia*]

*

p. 75: That, you will say, is a difficult conception. Well, so it is. But you know there was once a Spanish king who was shown how complicated the structure of the universe is. He thought he would have made it simpler.

The King was Alphons X (1252-1282), who was king of Castile. His statement is reported by Leibniz in his *Theodicy* (1710).

*

p. 76: Even the phantoms described by Schrenk-Notzing are only fine, physical exudations which retain in their shape traces of the etheric.

Albert Freiherr von Schrenk-Notzing (1862-1929) "was
a German physician, psychiatrist and notable psychical researcher, who
devoted his time to the study of paranormal events connected
with mediumship, hypnotism and telepathy…. He is credited as the
first forensic psychologist …" [*Wikipedia*]

On dreams generally: See the commentary.

Lecture 8

February 9, 1924

The title of this lecture translates literally: "Dreams and Imaginative Cognition: Guilt and the Foundation of Karma."

*

> *p. 111: If we can perceive the human being imaginatively, such a picture which we might attempt to paint will not be symbolic in the bad sense that symbolism has today. It will not be empty and insipid, but will contain elements of physical existence while, at the same time, transcending the physical.*

It seems from this and a number of other passages that Rudolf Steiner does not actually mean "symbolism," but rather allegory. Allegory is indeed insipid, but symbolism is not. It is somewhat ironic that a Goethe scholar of Steiner's stature would be a bit confused about the distinction, since it was Goethe who was the first to firmly distinguish symbol from allegory.

Lecture 9

February 10, 1924

The title of this lecture translates literally: "The Human Capacity for Memory."

*

p. 120: You have seen from the preceding lectures that a study of man's faculty of memory can give us valuable insight into the whole of human life and its cosmic connections. So today we will study this faculty of memory as such, in the various phases of its manifestation in human life, beginning with its manifestation in the ordinary consciousness that man has between birth and death.

See the Commentary for an extended discussion of memory.

*

p. 124: Now, I'm going backwards through our life, we do not undergo our experience, but his. We experience what he experienced through our deed. That, too, is part of the spiritual counterpart and is inscribed into the spiritual world. In short, man lives through his experiences once more, but in a spiritual way, going backwards from death to birth.

See Rudolf Steiner, *Karmic Relationships* 30, 31, and 38 ([Amazon:] Keryx, 2018-). See also Rudolf Steiner, GA 141; *Between Death and Rebirth: Ten Lecture Given in Berlin Between 5th November 1912 and 1st April 1913* (London: Rudolf Steiner Press, 1975); Rudolf Steiner, GA 153; *The Inner Nature of Man and Our Life Between Death and a New Birth*, translated by A. R. Meuss (1994; Forest Row: Rudolf Steiner House, 2013); and Rudolf Steiner, GA 231; *At Home in the Universe: Exploring our Suprasensory Nature.* (Hudson, New York: Anthroposophic Press, 2000).

*

p. 125: There are descriptions of this experience which, as I said yesterday, lasts one-third of the time of physical life, which depicted as a veritable hell.

63

Kamaloka is the period after death when the soul is freeing itself from its inclination toward physical existence in order to follow the laws of the spiritual world. See chapter 3 of CW 9; *Theosophy*, or chapter 3 of CW 13; *An Outline of Esoteric Science*. Of the Theosophical literature, see for example Annie Besant's description of *kamaloka* in *The Ancient Wisdom* (London, 1897).

Appendices

APPENDIX 1

EDITOR'S PREFACE

This book is the transcript of the shorthand report of nine lectures given by Rudolf Steiner in the early part of 1924, about a year before he died. Although his audience consisted very largely of people who had been studying for many years the spiritual science which is Steiner's legacy to the world (and which he also called *Anthroposophie*), he himself described the course as an "Introduction." The German title of the book is *Anthroposophie: Eine Einführung in die anthroposophische Weltanschauung.* "We will begin again," he observed in Lecture IV, "where we began 20 years ago"; and he may well have had in mind that the Movement itself had, in some sense, begun again only a month or two before with the solemn Foundation of the General Anthroposophical Society under himself as President at Christmas 1923. Though he proceeded *ab initio*,[3] assuming no previous knowledge on the part of his hearers, this course is not an elementary exposition of Anthroposophy. We are gradually led deeply in, and the path is steep towards the end.

There are many very different approaches to the general corpus of revelations or teachings which constitutes Spiritual Science. As with Nature herself, it is often only as the student penetrates deeper and nearer to the center that any connection between these different approaches becomes apparent. A reader of *Christianity As a Mystical Fact*,[4] for example, which dates from 1902, and of Steiner's lectures on the Gospels might well be surprised to find that it is possible to read *Theosophy* (1904) without ever discovering that the incarnation of Christ and the death on Golgatha are, according to him, the very core of the

---

[3] "from the beginning:" (Latin)

[4] CW 8; *Christianity as Mystical Fact and the Mysteries of Antiquity*, trans. Andrew Welburn, ed. Christopher Bamford (Great Barrington: SteinerBooks, 2006).

evolution of the universe and man. The truth is that the mastery of Anthroposophy involves, for our too stereotyped thinking, something like the learning of a new language. It would be possible to learn to read Greek and only afterwards to discover that the New Testament was written in that tongue.

From this point of view their present book is in the same category as *Theosophy*, yet even within this category the two approaches are made from such diverse directions that one might almost suppose the books to be the work of different men. Nevertheless it is best to look on the following lectures – as Steiner himself makes it clear that he does – as a supplement or complement to what is to be found in *Theosophy*.

The book *Theosophy* is the most systematic of all the writings that Steiner has bequeathed to us. Its whole basis is classification and definition and, taken by itself, it undoubtedly gives (quite apart from the dubious associations which the *word* "theosophy" has for English ears) a false impression of the nature of Anthroposophy. It is as indispensable to the student as a good grammar is indispensable to a man engaged in mastering a new language, and it contains as much – and as little – as a grammar does of all that the language can do and say. Its method is that of description from outside. And this approach, as substantial as it is as one among others, is perhaps the one most likely to lead to misunderstanding and misrepresentation. Such terms as "soul world," "spiritland," "elemental beings," "aura," are liable to be taken literally in spite of the author's express warnings to the contrary. The descriptions are taken as *reproductions* of the reality that underlies them instead of as similes – attempts, that is, at making clear a purely spiritual reality in words which have received their stamp of significance from their relation to the physical world.

No one who studies the teachings of Rudolf Steiner seriously remains in any real danger of succumbing to this sort of literalness. But anyone reading hurriedly through the book *Theosophy* – or even through *Theosophy* and the *Outline of Occult Science* – and inclined to judge the value of Anthroposophy from that single adventure may well do so. That is why the present book seems to me to be an important one – not only for "advanced" students of Anthroposophy, to whom it is perhaps primarily addressed, but also to the comparative beginner. It is condensed and difficult for most readers, and above all for those who have never dipped into the broad unbroken stream of books and lectures which flowed from Rudolf Steiner during the 20 years that elapsed between the publication of *Theosophy* and the delivery of this Course. But even if the content is far from fully understood, it cannot fail to give the reader some idea, let us say, of *the sort of thing* that is really signified by the spatial and other physical metaphors in which the systematic exposition of *Theosophy* is couched.

For here the approach is from within. It is no longer simply the objective facts and events, but the way in which the soul tentatively begins to experience these, which the lecturer makes such earnest efforts to convey. We have exchanged a guide for a book of travel. The one who is been there re-creates his experience for the benefit of those who have not, trying with every device at his disposal to reveal what it actually *felt* like. Of course the difficulty is still there; it can still only be done by metaphor and suggestion; but the difficulty is much less likely to be burked[5] by the reader's surreptitiously substituting in his own imagination a physical or sense-experience for a purely supersensible one.

Compare, for instance the description of the astral body given in *Theosophy* with the characterization of the in No. V of these lectures:

> [No. V] One says to oneself: What I am observing as the astral body of this person is not really present today, i.e. on 2nd February 1924. If the person is twenty years of age, you must go backwards in time – let us say, to January 1904. You perceive that this astral body is really back there, and extends still further back into the unlimited. It has remained

---

[5] An unusual legal term. It means literally to kill by suffocation and make it seem that the cause of death was of otherwise. Figuratively, it means to suppress quietly or indirectly.

there and has not accompanied him through the life. Here we have only a kind of appearance – a beam. Is like looking down and avenue; there, in the distance, are the last trees, very close together. Behind them is a source of light. You can have the radiance of the light *here*, but the source is behind – it need not move forward that it's light may shine here.

So, too, the astral body has remained behind, and only throws its beam into life. It has really remained in the spiritual world and has not come with us into the physical. In respect to our astral body we always remain before conception and birth, in the spiritual world. If we are twenty years old in 1924, it is as if we were still living spiritually before the year 1904 and, in respect to our astral body, had only stretched forth a feeler.

"Thus," he adds a few pages later, "if you describe the astral body as I have done in my *Theosophy* you must realise, *in order to complete your insight* (my italics)":

that what is active here is the "radiance" of something far back in time. The human being is really like a comet stretching its tail far back into the past. It is not possible to obtain a true insight into man's being unless we acquire these new concepts. People who believe one can enter the spiritual world with the same concepts one has for the physical world should become spiritualists, not anthroposophists.

In the same way one could compare the description of the etheric body in the earlier book with its treatment here in Lecture IV. The etheric body is not a vehicle of any such "life-force," as is understood by the creative evolutionists. It is totally incompatible with the assumptions of positivist science. If it can be described as a "formative forces" body, it can equally well be described, from another approach, as a thought-body. This is the approach which is required for all the teachings which Steiner developed later concerning the descent of the Cosmic Intelligence and its progressive embodiment in the personal intelligence of man. And it is this approach which is chosen in the book which follows.

He begins by describing the practical steps needed to develop the "strengthened thinking" which is the first stage of higher knowledge. And he continues:

> If you strengthen your thinking the supra-terrestrial spatial world begins to concern you and the "second man" you have discovered – just as the earthly, physical world concerned you before. And, as you ascribe the origin of your physical body to the physical earth, you now ascribe your second existence to the cosmic ether through whose activity earthly things become visible. From your own experience you can now speak of having a physical body *and an etheric body* … I stretch out my physical arm and my physical hand takes hold of an object. I feel in a sense the flowing forces in this action. Through strengthening my thought I come to feel that it is inwardly mobile and now induces a kind of "touching" within me – a "touching" that also takes place in an organism; this is the etheric organism; that finer, supersensible organism which exists no less than the physical organism, though it is connected with the supra-terrestrial, not the terrestrial.

Equally important is the exposition in this lecture of the way in which astral and etheric find outward expression in the *physical* constitution of man, the etheric in his fluid organization, which can only be understood with the help of the concept of the etheric body, and the astral in that "third man" – who is physically the "airy man" and who can be experienced as "an inner musical element in the breathing." The nervous system is shown to be the representation of this inner music.

The matter in this book is extremely condensed and one feels one is maiming it by arbitrary selections such as I am making for the purpose of this Introduction. I have, for instance, said nothing of the extensive and detailed discourse on dreams contained in Lectures VII and VIII, which some readers may even find the most enlightening thing in the book. One final selection may however perhaps be made. In these lectures Steiner approaches the life after death by speaking of "four phases of memory." The theme of these is first heard in Lecture VI, where, after speaking of the nature of memory he emphasizes that this is not the concern of the remembering individual alone, but is there for the sake of the universe – "in order that its content may pass through us and be received again in the forms into which we can transmute it."

> The universe needs us because, through us, it "fulfills" itself – fills itself again and again with its own content…. The universe gives its cosmic thoughts to our etheric body and receives them back again in a humanised condition.

It receives them back when we die. The moment we die, the world takes back what has given. "But it is something new that it receives, for we have experienced it all in a particular way." Then, in the ninth and last lecture, the last three phases of memory lead into – indeed become – in a miracle of condensation – all that is presented so differently in *Theosophy* under such titles as "The Soul in the Soul-World after Death."

Is this an esoteric or an exoteric work? Certainly it will be more readily appreciated by readers who have worked through other approaches to be found in the books and lecture-cycles and perhaps especially in the *Leading Thoughts*.[6] Yet it is the whole aim and character of Spiritual Science, as Rudolf Steiner developed it, to endeavor to be esoteric in an exoteric way. For that was what he believed the crisis of of the twentieth century demands. And I doubt if he ever struggled harder to combine the two qualities than in these nine lectures given at the end of his life. Thus, although he was addressing members of the Anthroposophical Society, I believe that he had his gaze

---

[6] See my new translation of this important text: GA 26; *Anthroposophical Leading Thoughts: The Cognitional Path of Anthroposophy – The Mystery of Michael.* Vols. 1-7. Ed. and trans. Frederick Amrine. ([Amazon:]) Keryx, 2019.

fixed on Western man in general, and I hope that an increasing number of those who are as yet unacquainted with any of his teaching may find in this book (and it can only be done by intensive application) a convincing proof of the immense fund of wisdom, insight and knowledge from which these teachings spring.

Owen Barfield

London,

August 1960

APPENDIX 2

Representation

Translators' introductions or notes invariably comment on the difficulty of translating *vorstellen/Vorstellung* and a few other German philosophical and psychological terms such as *Geist, Anschauung*, and *Gemüt*. Tellingly, the title of Schopenhauer's *magnum opus, Die Welt als Wille und Vorstellung*, has been three different ways: initially as "Representation," but then more recently as "Idea" and finally as "Presentation." Both Michael Wilson's translation of Steiner's *Philosophy of Freedom* and Owen Barfield's *The Case for Anthroposophy*[7] begin their discussions by noting that the standard translation of this Kantian philosophical term is "representation." But then Wilson goes on to argue (rightly) that this is too technical a term for most contexts, and that "representation" has other, distracting meanings

---

[7] This is older, partial translation. For a newer translation, see Rudolf Steiner, *CW 21; On The Enigmas of the Soul,* trans. Frederick Amrine and Owen Barfield, commentary by Frederick Amrine ([Amazon:] Keryx 2017).

outside of philosophy, which led him to translate *Vorstellung* and its variants as "mental picture." Barfield chooses "representation," which is understandable given that the context is Steiner's discussion of Brentano's neo-Kantian treatise. The reasons why this term is so very difficult to translate are (1) that it encompasses many different kinds of mental acts; (2) it refuses any sharp distinction between subjective and objective; (3) it can refer to a faculty, the activity of a faculty, or the result of that activity; (4) it often has a distinctly visual quality, but it can also refer to abstract concepts; and (5) it straddles the conventional divide between philosophy and psychology.

APPENDIX 3

The Etheric and the Astral Bodies

"Etheric body" is Steiner's early, theosophical term for the subtle body of supra-physical forces that sustains life. Later he would also refer to it variously as "the life body," or the "formative forces body," or (echoing Spinoza's distinction between *natura naturans* and *natura naturata*) the realm of "living working" as opposed to the physical realm of "finished work." The etheric body is precipitated out of a vast cosmic ether. It is known through Imaginaton, and first reveals itself to strengthened thinking as supra-sensible pictures. The etheric body consists of centrifugal forces, expresses itself in all aqueous processes, and flows in great currents through the cosmos. The etheric is a "time body"; here time becomes space. It is a unity that is always there as a temporal totality, right up to the present moment. Theodor Schwenk's *Sensitive Chaos: The Creation of Flowing Forms in Water and Air*

(London: Rudolf Steiner Press, 1996) is a scientifically compelling and aesthetically beautiful exploration of these forces.

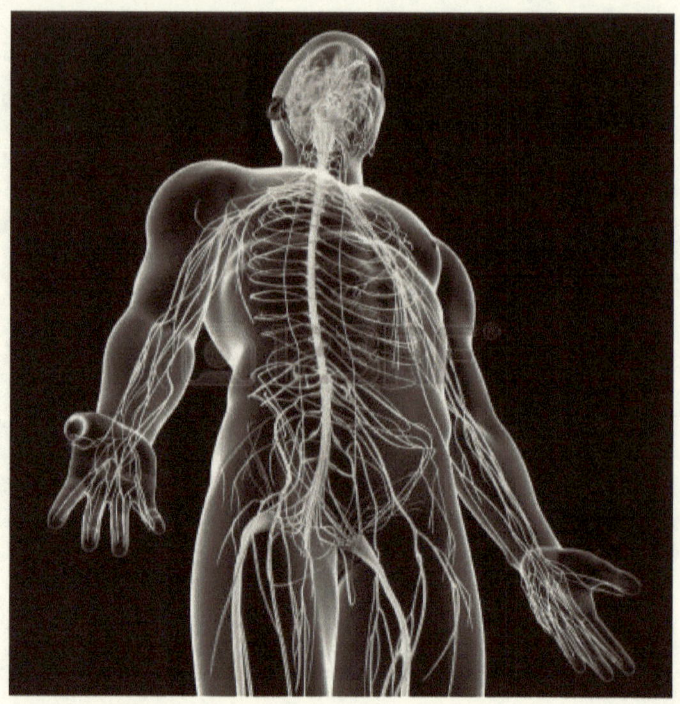

"Astral body" is Steiner's early, theosophical term for the subtle body that corresponds generally to "soul" or "psyche." Like Freud and Jung, he sees it as internally differentiated and gradually transformed by the activity of the higher faculty of the "I" or "ego." The astral body reveals itself to Inspiration, and emerges in a sense from behind Imagination. The traditional concept of the Music of the Spheres is an experience of macrocosmic astrality. It consists of centripetal forces, and expresses itself in breathing and in the airy element generally. It also expresses itself as the human nervous system. The astral body has remained behind in time, and casts its beams forward into the present incarnation; it remains in the spiritual world before conception and birth

The *locus classicus* for both of these bodies among Steiner's introductory works is the uncharacteristically schematic and static description in his early book *Theosophy* (1904; many English editions are available, including now a very inexpensive Kindle Edition from Amazon). A much more dynamic (but also much more difficult) account is to be found in the middle four lectures of Rudolf Steiner, *A Psychology of Body, Soul, & Spirit* (New York: SteinerBooks, 1999), which includes a valuable introduction by Robert Sardello. See also Lecture 5 (February 2, 1924) of the cycle GA 234; *Anthroposophy: An Introduction*, trans. and intro. Owen Barfield (London: Anthroposophical Publishing Co., 1961).